Missional
Analysis of
Peoples
Places
Interests
Needs &
Godliness

Rev. Chris McNairy
7/17/2015

Rev. Chris McNairy

1

Urban

Fusion

Network

Planting the Gospel... "Together"

Books

Missional Analysis of Peoples, Places, Interests, Needs, and Godliness ®

How mission field contexts help inform what God would have us to do individually and collaboratively.

Unless otherwise noted, all Scripture quotations are taken from the King James Version of the Bible. Other versions used where noted are also from the Bible Gateway. www.biblegateway.com

Urban Fusion Network Books

P.O. Box 2227 Lawrenceville, Georgia 30046

ISBN-13: 978-0989591225

ISBN-10: 0989591220

Dedication

Dedicated to all those who have prayed for me. Especially those who continue to pray for me regularly. I recognize that no man is an island. God has made us to be interdependent.

Table of Contents

Acknowledgement .... Page 8

Introduction.. Page 9

Chapter 1 – M.A.P.P.I.N.G. A Biblical Example .... Page 15

Chapter 2 – M.A.P.P.I.N.G. Prayer ....Page 20

Chapter 3 – M.A.P.P.I.N.G. Peoples and Places..........Page 36

Chapter 4 – M.A.P.P.I.N.G. Interests and Needs........Page 59

Chapter 5 – M.A.P.P.I.N.G. A Godliness Barometer...Page 67

Appendix.. Page 80

- Sources of information
- Jerusalem Survey template
- Jerusalem Vision Tour over-view
- Local Church Jerusalem Check list
- Missional Scorecard Over-view
- Glossary of Relevant Terms

About the Author..Page 94

Conferences Offered by Chris McNairy....................... Page 95

Endnotes... Page 97

Acknowledgement

Hold to God's Unchanging Hand[i]

Time is filled with swift transition,

Naught of earth unmoved can stand,

Build your hopes on things eternal,

Hold to God's unchanging hand.

Trust in Him who will not leave you,

Whatsoever years may bring,

If by earthly friends forsaken

Still more closely to Him cling.

Covet not this world's vain riches

That so rapidly decay,

Seek to gain the heav'nly treasures,

They will never pass away.

When your journey is completed,

If to God you have been true,

Fair and bright the home in glory

Your enraptured soul will view.

Refrain:

Hold to God's unchanging hand, Hold to God's unchanging hand;

Build your hopes on things eternal,

Hold to God's unchanging hand.

Introduction

Kingdom workers of all types need an approach to generally analyzing mission fields and local field workers need a process that helps them exegete their Jerusalem for developing and implementing missional strategies. What might this look like?

- Prayer through various venues (Core 20-30 hours) and ongoing.
- Information Gathering (10-20 work hours)
- Surveying (12 – 15 work hours)
- Analysis (3-5 work hours)
- Development of Key Strategy Components (1-3 work hours)
- Presentation of Findings (1 hour+ more if spirited discussion)
- Joining God (A Lifetime)

God's Word, Prayer, Mission field research and analysis should inform missional strategy. That's why it is important to prayerfully consider the mission field for accurate context and change on a regular basis. We should do evangelism and missions based on current realities and projected trends as understood through the power of the Holy Spirit.

MAPPING – as I present it is an acrostic for **M**issional **A**nalysis of **P**eople **P**laces **I**nterests **N**eeds and **G**odliness. **MAPPING** is a process, based on Numbers 13, that I have personally used over the years to understand various field context in missionary service. I have applied this mission field understanding approach to my individual ministry, local church settings, as well as regional and national contexts. **MAPPING** is a contributory means towards an end. It is not the end. The end is the reconciliation of men, women, boys and girls to God through the planting of the Gospel as they live out transformed lives.

The book of Numbers has impacted my discipleship journey in three major areas:

- The sovereignty of God
- Biblical foundations for missional research and analysis. This work is centered in this area. Principally Numbers 13.
- Biblical principles for Leadership especially shared leadership.

Just in case you are reading this book and don't have a relationship with God through Jesus Christ as your Lord and Savior (not a disciple). Consider the following:[ii]

John 3:16 (KJV)
For God so loved the world, that he gave his only begotten Son, that whosoever believeth in him should not perish, but have everlasting life.

Everyone needs to be loved. Some may feel that they are not worthy to be loved by God or need to somehow make themselves better in order to be loved by God.

Here's what God says: ...God directed his love toward us, in that, while we were yet sinners, Christ died for us. Romans 5:8

A tangible way of showing love is by giving. Heaven is a gift from God. Every gift has three attributes.

- A Giver
- A Purchaser
- A Receiver

As John 3:16 shares, God is the Giver. In 1 Peter 1:18-19, we are reminded that Jesus is the purchaser.

[18] Forasmuch as ye know that ye were not redeemed with corruptible things, *as* silver and

gold... [19] but with the precious blood of Christ, as of a lamb without blemish and without spot:...

What completes the gift of Heaven is our accepting it. Have you received your free gift of Heaven? If not, then sincerely pray:

Jesus, I thank you for loving me and dying for me. I want to accept your love. I ask for your forgiveness. I turn from my sinful life and welcome your control of my life. I place my trust in you and you alone for everlasting life. Thank you Jesus for giving me new life.

Congratulations!!! Your decision to become a part of God's family is the **most important decision** you will ever make.

What now?

- **Tell** someone who will be happy about your decision.
- **Talk** to God daily.
- **Read** the Bible daily.
- **Become** a part of a Bible believing church.
- **Grow** in being more like Jesus daily.

Demographic reports that are purchased or freely given and various information dumping are much less impactful on missionaries and leaders than a MAPPING process that informs missional strategy and singes the burden of the mission field on the hearts of these people.   Missional research should not be delegated. It should be engaged.

Defining missional...
The processes, patterns, principles, and practices through which disciples with a biblical worldview join God in his mission of building his kingdom of transformed Christ followers.

What might be involved in a **MAPPING** Process?

- Prayerfully understanding the parameters of an area
- History of the area
- Strategic windshield surveying during at least three different days and different times of day. In addition, urban areas or larger can be viewed on Google Earth and one can literally prayer walk the streets at their computer or tablet. Google does regular updates of the site.
- Already compiled information from various local field sources (local-state-national government entities, Chamber of Commerce, community agencies, Schools districts, colleges and universities).
- What are other evangelical Kingdom partners are already doing?
- Recent photographs and videos of field information/people. The internet, smart phones and tablets make this much easier.
- Most recent community projection information

What are those things that are part of a current reality, no matter how difficult to handle, that must be confronted? Apply this question to your local situation and the broader American mission field.

> # Stubborn Facts
> We are entitled to our own opinions (whatever they may be); but we are not entitled to our own facts.

Analyzing your findings

- Know that interpretation is not neutral. Try to always have more than one set of eyes look at the area of focus.
- Fully digest the information (Proverbs 4:7)
- Previous conversations and field engagement should not be forgotten.
- Reflect about the personal meaning of any information received.

- Compare and contrast personal viewpoints with the various information findings.
- Know the limitations of the information findings.
- Consider what future research might look like.

Anticipated Outcomes of any MAPPING Process:

- Confirming of research data that is easily available
- Detailed informing of missional strategy development and implementation
- Informing profiles of types of missionaries needed.
- Identifying local urban influencers.
- Prepare for urban area media Gospel planting saturation.

We should never do missional research and analysis to place a notebook on the shelf and check it off as an activity on a to-do list. In as much as God already knows, we must position ourselves to know what he would have us to know so that we can do what he would have us do.

God has not given us a spirit of fear. We should not be overwhelmed at any level by the composition, rapid changes, and diversity of the present age. God is concerned with every person. Every soul.

Chapter One
M.A.P.P.I.N.G.
A Biblical Example

And the Lord spoke to Moses, saying, "Send men to spy out the land of Canaan, which I am giving to the children of Israel; from each tribe of their fathers you shall send a man, everyone a leader among them." So Moses sent them from the Wilderness of Paran according to the command of the Lord, all of them men who *were* heads of the children of Israel.   Numbers 13:1-3 NKJV

Canaan can be seen as an example of the kingdom of God; the wilderness through which the Israelites passed, of the difficulties and trials to be met with in the present world. The promise of the kingdom of God is given to every believer; but how many are discouraged by the difficulties in the way! A faithless heart sees dangers, lions, and giants, everywhere; and therefore refuses to proceed in the heavenly path. Many of the faithless heart spies contribute to this by the bad reports they bring of the heavenly country. Some preachers and teachers allow "that the land is good, that it flows with milk and honey," and go so far as to show some of its fruits; but they discourage the people by stating the impossibility of overcoming their enemies. "Sin," say they, "cannot be destroyed in this life-it will always dwell in you.

> The *Anakim* cannot be conquered-we are but as grasshoppers against the Anakim," Joshua and a Caleb, trusting alone in the power of God, armed with faith in the infinite efficacy of that blood which cleanses from all unrighteousness, boldly stand forth and say: "Their defense is departed from them, and the Lord is with us; let us go up at once and possess the land, for we are well able to overcome."

We can do all things through Christ strengthening us: he will purify us unto himself, and give us that rest from sin here which his death has procured and his word has promised. Reader, can we not take God at his word? He has never failed us. Surely then we have no reason to doubt. We have not even tried him to the extent he can be tried. While we know he can save, we don't know how far and how fully he can save. We should know there is no limit to his salvation. Don't be depressed; the sons of Anak shall fall before thee, if thou meet them in the name of the LORD of HOSTS.

A kingdom movement (or segment of a movement) at any level can only be quantified by an accurate depiction of the starting point. In analysis we show to what extent we accept reality and set a preferred future. You will only know if you are having impact if you pointed to a reality when starting. It is quite telling when the same number of lost figures are used over decades of quantification, in some cases as a badge of honor. Data is unrelentingly stubborn and when faced head on cannot be manipulated.

> Then Moses sent them to spy out the land of Canaan, and said to them, "Go up this *way* into the South, and go up to the mountains, [18] and see what the land is like: whether the people who dwell in it *are* strong or weak, few or many; [19] whether the land they dwell in *is* good or bad; whether the cities they inhabit *are* like camps or strongholds; [20] whether the land *is* rich or poor; and whether there are forests there or not. Be of good courage. And bring some of the fruit of the land." Now the time *was* the season of the first ripe grapes.   Numbers 13:17-20 (NKJV)

Verse 17 –This promise land (a gift from God) had only to be possessed. Examining the land should have been akin to examining a gift from a box after opening it For me when I open a gift it is no longer a matter of possessing it, I excitedly possess it. Unfortunately, there were questions in the minds of ten of those sent to spy the land. A research assignment is given to understand this promise land gift.

- The Focus area (Land of Canaan) is defined.
- Markers identified (From the valley to the mountain)

Verse 18 – Geographic lay-out (natural barriers) to be examined.

Identify the people (Demographic, psychographic and worldview studies)

Verse 19 – How are the cities (places) set up? (Large dense or sparse areas)

Are the communities' single or multi-family housing? Gated?

Verse 20 – What is the economy like? Is the area self –propagating?   Is there

Agriculture? Timber? Indicators of how the people build structures.

Fruit? Crops? What are the indicators of how the people eat (fellowship)?

In 21st century terms Moses in Numbers 13 gives a missional research assignment. The Focus area (Land of Canaan) is defined. The more exact parameters are identified (From the valley to the mountain). This is the where. Beginning in verse 18 the spies are told to examine place. Place is an important impact in how we do life. Place in America impacts sub-cultural world views. The geographic lay-out (natural barriers) was to be examined and they were to identify the peoples in the place. (Demographic studies) How are the cities set up? (Large and dense or sparse areas) Are the communities composed of single family housing or multi-family housing? Gated? What is the economy like? Is the area self –propagating? Is there agriculture? Timber? Are these indicators of how the people build common (community) structures?   What are the fruit and crops like? Foods are indicative of how the people eat (fellowship). Then they told him, and said:

> "We went to the land where you sent us. It truly flows with milk and honey, and this *is* its fruit. ²⁸ Nevertheless the people who dwell in the land *are* strong; the cities *are* fortified *and* very large; moreover we saw the descendants of Anak there. ²⁹ The Amalekites dwell in the land of the South; the Hittites, the Jebusites, and the Amorites dwell in the mountains; and the Canaanites dwell by the sea and along the banks of the Jordan." ³⁰ Then Caleb quieted the people before Moses, and said, "Let us go up at once and take possession, for we are well able to overcome it." Numbers 13:27-30 (NKJV)

Verse 27 – Connecting report with area assigned...

- Verify some assumptions.... Dispel others....
- Wealth and poverty of the area identified
- Visual evidence of what is being reported.

Verse 28 – Profile of the neighbourhoods/communities that make up the area. Profiles of the people (s) that stand out or that are familiar.

Verse 29 – Initial broad identification of the Peoples. Insight into history and world-view of current residents.

Verse 30 – Immediate response to MAPPING. Caleb's sense of urgency and purpose.

In Numbers 13:27 the spies report on the area assigned. Wealth and poverty of the area are identified. They verified some assumptions and dispelled others. In addition the spies brought visual evidence of what is being reported. In addition the profile of the neighborhoods/communities making up the area as well as profiles of the peoples that stand out or are historically familiar. The immediate positive response to MAPPING is Caleb's sense of urgency and purpose. This should be our response to God's revelation through prayer and missional research/analysis. We should have an obedient spirit knowing that God is able to do exceedingly abundantly above anything we can ask or think. In America we should come to expect diversity to be encountered as we engage the mission field. As we go about making disciples, diversity is a good thing.

A 4-P look at ethno-cultural inclusiveness:

- The Past – Other peoples have a history worth sharing.
- The Present – Other peoples' participation is worth having.
- The Perspective – Other peoples have thinking worth discussing.
- The Prophetic – Other peoples' have Godly revelation that is not to be ignored.

Chapter Two
M.A.P.P.I.N.G. and Prayer

…Your kingdom come. Your will be done on earth as *it is* in heaven.   Matthew 6:10 NKJV

Prayer

Little Prayer = Little Power;
Some Prayer = Some Power;
Much Prayer = Much Power!

While serving as a Pastor in Memphis, Tennessee in the 1990s I had a placard outside of my office that said "If God deems prayer so essential why is it that we do so little of it? Expect to pray when you enter.

The most important strategy we can implore in any situation is to carry out a prayer focus. Prayer is not part of the strategy, it is the strategy. It is not part of the battle, it is the battle.

.

The early church in the book of Acts is a great biblical model of a prayer strategy.

Acts 1:13-15 states... And when they were come in, they went up into an upper room, where abode both Peter, and James, and John, and Andrew, Philip, and Thomas, Bartholomew, and Matthew, James the son of Alphaeus, and Simon Zelotes, and Judas the brother of

James. These all continued with one accord in prayer and supplication, with the women, and Mary the mother of Jesus, and with his brethren. And in those days Peter stood up in the midst of the disciples, and said, (the number of names together were about an hundred and twenty,)

120 prayed and impacted 3000 for the Kingdom. Today we get all excited when 3000 impact 120. Has God changed? No, but we seem to have elevated man's traditions and success models above God's word and way. Let's pray that God's work will be done his way with the results he desires.

Acts 2:41-42 states:

> Then they that gladly received his word were baptized: and the same day there were added unto them about three thousand souls. And they continued steadfastly in the apostles' doctrine and fellowship, and in breaking of bread, and in prayers.

There is a proportional relationship between how important things are to believers and the frequency and fervor that the believer brings things to the Father. How serious are we about reaching the lost and making Disciples in out Jerusalem?

One of the vast areas of lostness in America are its ever increasing multihousing communities. We need to pray specifically for those who are literally the gatekeepers for millions of residents in the multihousing communities of America. The majority of the residents of these communities are unchurched. The planting of the Gospel in multihousing communities starts with focused prayer for owners and managers of the multihousing communities in your area. This prayer time is not pre-ministry, it is ministry.

Pray for Public Officials

We need to pray for our local, state, regional, and national public officials. The question is are we? Prayer for public officials is not a political issue. In fact if we do feel that a public official is wrong in their public policy prayer is the Christians greatest weapon.

We need to pray for public officials. Why? God's word directs us to.

> [1]I exhort therefore, that, first of all, supplications, prayers, intercessions, and giving of thanks, be made for all men; [2]For kings, and for all that are in authority; that we may lead a quiet and peaceable life in all godliness and honesty. [3]For this is good and acceptable in the sight of God our Saviour; 1 Timothy 2:1-3

We need to pray for public officials because God is in control of everything including government.

> The king's heart is in the hand of the LORD, as the rivers of water: he turneth it whithersoever he will. Proverbs 21:1

What a tremendous word from the Lord. His power is awesome and there is no failure in him. We should learn if we are not already doing it how to pray the scriptures. Prayer is not optional….

A.S.K. – Ask, Seek and Knock

We only know what to do through prayer, missional research and analysis on a foundation of God's word.

We all need prayer and one of the ways we model dependence on prayer is by sharing how people can pray for us. This can be humbling as we are transparent. I always bring my prayer concerns to groups and/or churches when meeting, conferencing or preaching.

At any given time I try to have an answer if only verbally to the following three questions:

1) What are my top five personal prayer concerns?

2) What are my top five prayer/resource needs for ministry?

3) What are my top five personal needs?

> And I say unto you, Ask, and it shall be given you; seek, and ye shall find; knock, and it shall be opened unto you. For every one that asketh receiveth; and he that seeketh findeth; and to him that knocketh it shall be opened. If a son shall ask bread of any of you that is a father, will he give him a stone? or if he ask a fish, will he for a fish give him a serpent? Or if he shall ask an egg, will he offer him a scorpion? If ye then, being evil, know how to give good gifts unto your children: how much more shall your heavenly Father give the Holy Spirit to them that ask him? (Luke 11:9-13

We have not because we ask (Ask Seek Knock) not. Maintain a mental or hard copy answer to all three questions at all times. Keep it real. Some people genuinely want to and will pray for you regularly and many times on a daily basis.   Other people love to and will give to the support of your ministry. Still others want to share directly to you and your family. Don't let pride and/or a false sense of humility hinder blessings.

Reference James 5:13-18.

> Is any among you afflicted? Let him pray. Is any merry? Let him sing psalms. Is any sick among you? Let him call for the elders of the church; and let them pray over him, anointing him with oil in the name of the Lord: is and the prayer of faith shall save the sick, and the Lord shall raise him up; and if he have committed sins, they shall be forgiven him. Confess your faults one to another, and pray one for another, that ye may be healed. The effectual fervent prayer of a righteous man availeth much. Elias was a man subject to like passions as we are, and he prayed earnestly that it might not rain: and it rained not on the earth by the space of three years and

six months. And he prayed again, and the heaven gave rain, and the earth brought forth her fruit.

In Matthew 17:14-21 we find the account of the Father who brings his son to disciples but Jesus has to handle the situation when they fail to see a change in the young boy's condition. Jesus uses the teachable moment to emphasize prayer and fasting.

> And when they were come to the multitude, there came to him a certain man, kneeling down to him, and saying, Lord, have mercy on my son: for he is lunatick, and sore vexed: for ofttimes he falleth into the fire, and oft into the water. And I brought him to thy disciples, and they could not cure him. Then Jesus answered and said, O faithless and perverse generation, how long shall I be with you? how long shall I suffer you? bring him hither to me. And Jesus rebuked the devil; and he departed out of him: and the child was cured from that very hour. Then came the disciples to Jesus apart, and said, Why could not we cast him out? And Jesus said unto them, Because of your unbelief: for verily I say unto you, If ye have faith as a grain of mustard seed, ye shall say unto this mountain, Remove hence to yonder place; and it shall remove; and nothing shall be impossible unto you. Howbeit this kind goeth not out but by prayer and fasting.

Not only should we pray until something happens (P.U.S.H.); sometimes we must pray and fast. Do you want to see what God sees??? Do you want to know what God is doing in your ministry field? Do you really want to know where God wants you to join him??   Pray... PRAY... PRAY!!!   I am convinced that one of the most under used promises in scripture regarding church ministry is Matthew 9:37-38:

> Then saith he unto his disciples, The harvest truly is plenteous, but the labourers are few; Pray ye therefore the Lord of the harvest, that he will send forth labourers into his harvest.

Let's pray this scripture right now and every day until the Lord returns!!!

God knows the lost exist. After all, he did come to earth to die for all. He knows them by name and he wants us to get to know them also to bring them out of darkness into the marvelous light. If I have learned anything about enlisting workers for and from the harvest; I have learned that recruiting does not work. When I recruit people that I think can do the work, I fail. When I pray for wisdom in letting God send forth laborers it always succeeds.

If God deems PRAYER so essential, Why is it that we do so little of it?

A Biblical Basis for Missional Prayer

The only way we know where to go is to pray. The only way we know what to do is to pray. The only way we know when to go is to pray. The only way we know how we should go is to pray. Without out prayer we are only taking stabs in the darkness. We cannot be missional or on mission without prayer.

> But Jesus responded to them, "My Father is still working, and I also am working." Then Jesus replied, "I assure you: The Son is not able to do anything on His own, but only what He sees the Father doing. For whatever the Father does, these things the Son also does in the same way. For the Father loves the Son and shows Him everything He is doing, and he will show Him greater works than these so that you will be amazed. Selected portions from John 5:17-20 (HCSB)

> "I am the true vine, and My Father is the vineyard keeper. Remain in me, and I in you. Just as a branch is unable to produce fruit by itself unless it remains on the vine, so neither can you unless you remain in me. "I am the vine; you are the branches. The one who remains in me and I in him produces much fruit, because you can do nothing without Me. If anyone does not remain in me, he is thrown

aside like a branch and he withers. They gather them, throw them into the fire, and they are burned. If you remain in me and My words remain in you, ask whatever you want and it will be done for you. My Father is glorified by this: that you produce much fruit and prove to be my disciples.   Selected portions from John 15:1-8 (HCSB)

[18] Then Jesus came near and said to them, "All authority has been given to me in heaven and on earth. [19] Go, therefore, and make disciples of all nations, baptizing them in the name of the Father and of the Son and of the Holy Spirit, [20] teaching them to observe everything I have commanded you. And remember, I am with you always, to the end of the age."   Matthew 28:18-20 (HCSB)

Seeking God for Spiritual Awakening

Believing that we can do nothing of eternal consequence of on our own, and desiring to be a useful vessel through which God can extend His love and grace to the lost among all peoples we must be committed to intentionally engage in strategic missional prayer activities for spiritual awakening to occur in our Jerusalem, Judaea, Samaria, and the uttermost parts of the world. We can and should join in earnestly pleading to the Father that the millions of lost people across the land will be transformed by the good news of the gospel, in which the very power of God resides for all who believe.

Prayer reasserts the specific promises of God and for purposes of the local church Jerusalem informs the questions of where, what, how, and when.

Prayer[iii]

Components of Prayer

- Adoration
- Confession
- Thanksgiving
- Supplication
- Intercession
- Petition - Effective Prayer is not necessarily loud, long, or melodious.

Ten Reasons to Prayer

- To spend time with God. (The one you Love)
- To identify with God by becoming more like him.
- To identify with God by working together with him.
- To gain strength for resisting temptation.
- To be made right with God.
- To find forgiveness, mercy, and grace.
- To learn God's will.
- To offer sacrifices to God.
- To learn and obey authority.
- To release God's power

Tools That Assist in Praying Effectively

- Bible
- A written prayer list
- Hymnal or Song Book
- Prayer Journal
- Good Devotional Guide

Major Sin That Hinders Prayer

- Anger/Wrath – 1 Timothy 2:8
- Broken Relationship(s) – Matthew 5:23-24; 1 Peter 3:7
- Doubting/Unbelief – 1 Timothy 2:8

- Hypocrisy – Matthew 6:5
- Idolatry – Ezekiel 14:3
- Indifference to Need – Proverbs 21:13
- Unforgiveness – Matthew 6:14-15

How Do We Pray In Unity of The Spirit?

- Get into agreement with God…. (WWJD – What Would Jesus Do?)
- Get into agreement with others whom you are praying with.
- Seek God's (The Father's) perspective… Pray his will to be done

Principles of Asking In Personal Prayer

- Ask in the spirit – Ephesians 6:18
- Ask according to God's will – 1 John 5:14-15
- Ask with the right mind – 1 Corinthians 14:15
- Ask in Jesus name – John 14:14
- Ask while abiding in Christ – John 15:7
- Ask in faith – Mark 11:22,24
- Ask in humility – 2 Chronicles 7:14
- Ask in sincerity – James 5:16
- Ask with perseverance – Ephesians 6:18

What Does Asking Others To Pray For You Do?

- Shows dependence on God.
- Demonstrates lowliness before God and humility before others.
- Brings greater authority to prayer.
- Increases the amount of praying in your behalf.
- Broadens understanding of how to pray for your need(s).
- Blesses those who have the privilege of praying for you.
- Strengthens the bond of love between you and those who pray for you.
- Can secure strength for an area of personal weakness or failure

Fasting and Prayer

Fasting – A working definition:

The voluntary abstinence for a time from any necessity of life, person, thing, or activity that we hold dear.; such as food, drink, rest, sleep, people, television, telephone, etc. What makes the Christian fast different is its aim. The aim of Christian fasting is to improve one's relationship with God (The Soverign Father)

How long of a fast???

The time may vary depending on many dynamics.

Fasting from food and drink may not be for everyone at all times.

Christians with certain physical conditions may aggravate the condition with an extended fast and should seek medical advice before a dietary fast is undertaken.

Fasting – Usages in the Bible (origin of the word)

The word "fast" is found 75 times in the Bible. 44 times in the Old Testament from the Hebrew word "Tsoon" meaning to cover the mouth and 31 times in the New Testament from the Greek word "Nacetis" meaning not to eat. Many Bible scholars have identified Isaiah 58 as the Bible's most involved look at fasting.

Why Fast???

- The fast that God honors enables us to root out selfishness. Selfishness destroys our effectiveness with God and Man. As we receive inner liberation from sin and self we can help others.

- The fast that God honors examines the heart, admits personal problems, and receives the solution for these problems.
- The fast that God honors prepares us for sacrificial giving because we first gain from the discipline of self-denial. Our minds are off self and we are able to reorder our priorities, being better able to see the needs of others.
- The fast that God honors provides for physical purging and healing allowing God to make physical adjustments in our body through spiritual submission to him.

Some lengths of fasts in the Bible:

- Short period – 1 Corinthians 7:5
- One day – Judges 20:26
- Twice a week – Luke 18:12
- Seven days – 1 Samuel 31:13
- Fourteen days – Acts 27:33
- Forty Days (regular) – Matthew 4:2
- Forty Days (Supernatural) – Exodus 34:28

What about conduct during a fast???

- Make God and his will your focus.
- Give the devil no place.
- Seek God through prayer and meditation on his word as much as possible.
- Follow Matthew 6:16-20 (Don't fast for show)

What Biblical Fasts Produced???

- Frustration – Isaiah 58:3
- The will of God – Judges 20:26
- Hunger – Luke 4:1-2
- Victory – Matthew 4:2B-4
- Special Power for Difficult Tasks – Matthew 17:18-21

- Vision – Acts Chapter 10 (Cornelius and Peter)
- God's will in ordaining leaders – Acts 13:1-3; Acts 14:23
- Obvious presence of God's Spirit and Angels – Matthew 4:2-4, 11

SCRIPTURE	PERSON/PEOPLE INVOLVED	PURPOSE OF FAST
Exodus 34:27-28	Moses	10 Commandments
Judges 20:26	Israelites	Deliverance from enemies
1 Samuel 7:5-6	Samuel/Israelites	Repentance
1 Samuel 31:13	Men of Israel	Grief/Fear
II Samuel 1:11-12	David	Grief/ Lost of Love one
II Samuel 12:21-23	David	Preparation/Strength
1 Kings 19:2-8	Elijah	Special work of the Lord.
Nehemiah 1:4	Nehemiah	Rebuilding of wall.
Daniel 9:3-4	Daniel	For his society
Jonah 3:5	People of Nineveh	Repentance
Luke 2:36-37	Anna	Serve with power

Prayer Walking Over-view

What does prayer walking do?

Prayer walking is an up close and personal time with God that reveals how he is engaging the culture. During prayer walking God's vision is revealed, where he is at work is unfolded and the ministry field gets to experience the visible church of the Lord Jesus Christ up close and personal.

Determine the area to be covered

It still surprises me how many church leaders much less church members don't know what is their designated ministry field (Jerusalem). If you aim at nothing you will hit it every time. Focused prayer should be on a focus area. "And I will give unto thee the keys of the kingdom of heaven: and whatsoever thou shalt bind on earth shall be bound in heaven: and whatsoever thou shalt loose on earth shall be loosed in heaven." (Matthew 16:19 AV)

Set times when actual prayer walks will take place.

While the time for prayer walking should be consistent the area covered may be different. The more you prayer walk the ministry field the more the Holy Spirit will lead in where to go.

Who can/should participate?

Whoever is available and committed to the cause of Christ should participate. There is no limit to the ways God can and does use those who avail themselves.

Dressing for success

Prayer walking is not the time to wear your best dress shoes nor your most expensive suit or dress. It is a time to dress for the occasion. Modest conservative comfortable dress with as little jewelry as possible will go a long way toward getting you through even the toughest of areas.

What do I actually do while on a prayer walk?

Maintain a prayerful spirit and seek to be spiritually conscious of what is going on. When talking to those you walk with try to keep the conversation focused on what you see God doing and desiring to do. What do you see in the area that was hidden before? What burden does god seem to be impressing on your heart? What, if any, actions is God saying take immediately?

Informal and Formal debriefing:

Sharing with those you walk with while in the field is informal debriefing as is gathering with others who have prayer walked during same time period to share what God has revealed. A more formal debriefing can take place through prayer breakfasts or some other prayer fellowship meal.

Sharing testimonies with those beyond the prayer walking team:

God will always do what only God can do. You can count on God to provide you with compelling exciting testimonies to share with others. My experience has taught me to not only share verbally but to write the testimonies as much as possible so the impact can be as wide spread as possible.

In addition to prayer walking there is the urban phenomenon of "prayer drive-bys." We can ride a neighborhood, drive down a street or up to a multihousing community and zap the community with prayer. Driving off, in most cases, before anyone even knows we have been in the area. Prayer drive-bys are carried out just like prayer walks but involve vehicles.   Traffic laws should always be obeyed.

Chapter Three
M.A.P.P.I.N.G.
Peoples and Places

Then they told him, and said: "We went to the land where you sent us. It truly flows with milk and honey, and this *is* its fruit. Nevertheless the people who dwell in the land *are* strong; the cities *are* fortified *and* very large; moreover we saw the descendants of Anak there. The Amalekites dwell in the land of the South; the Hittites, the Jebusites, and the Amorites dwell in the mountains; and the Canaanites dwell by the sea and along the banks of the Jordan."

Numbers 13:27-29 NKJV

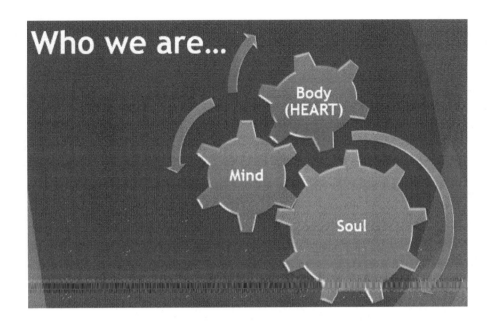

We must have the worldview conversation that essential shapes our missiology. Missiology being the way we essentially carry out the one mission of God. Worldview missiology cannot be considered the same as commonly held people group missiology. Most accept the word "worldview" as having German roots. A worldview is a person's mental concept of the "big picture" of reality as shaped by beliefs and assumptions about God, creation, humanity, morality, and purpose. A worldview is a comprehensive framework of beliefs that helps us to interpret what we see and experience. It also gives us direction in the choices we make as we live out our lives. Worldview is the lens or grid through which we interpret the world, the universe, and every percept of what is right or wrong with a person, family units, cultures, and nations.

Worldview Foundation Questions

- Is there a God and if so, how do I see him and relate to him?
- What makes for reality?
- Is there a reason and purpose for my existence?
- Who am I and How did I get here?
- How do I determine right and wrong?
- To whom do I ultimately answer?

In classical people group missiology, we segment people primarily by ethno linguistic categories. This type of segmentation and assumption regarding the thinking (worldviews) of peoples is not effective in 21st century America. This approach to understanding the mission field works well in tribal or agrarian societies but in urban fusion America it sets up a faulty foundation. If classical people segmentation were accurate in 21st century America the following ethno-linguistic pairings would be identical.

African – President Barack Obama and Supreme Court Justice Clarence Thomas do not have the same worldview.

Latino – Supreme Court Justice Sonia Sotomayor and United States Senator Marco Rubio do not have the same worldview.

Asian - Gary Locke who became the first Chinese American Secretary of Commerce and Bobby Jindal the governor of Louisiana do not have the same worldview.

European - Former Presidents George W. Bush and William Jefferson Clinton do not have the same worldview.

Jewish - Mark Zuckerberg (Facebook) and Eric Cantor Majority leader United States House of representatives do not have the same worldview.

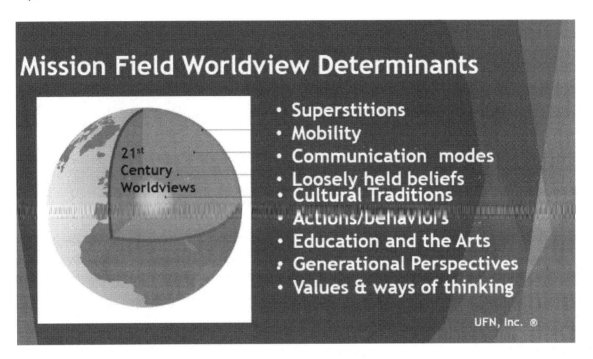

With ethnic, cultural, socio-economic, educational, gender, and other lens; outside of a relationship with God we have our own views and live on our own in a cold world. A sinners job description is to sin. From superstitions to salvation of works that guides good values and thinking mission field worldviews cannot be the foundation for disciples. Only the Biblical worldview from God's word is the solid foundation. Languages and Foods, while they can be indicators are not world view determinants. Fads ... come and go but are the result of world views not world view determinants.

In the Gospel of Luke, Jesus used a fishing backdrop to teach the disciples a Gospel planting lesson. The Christian church today should apply the same principles, especially as we consider the peoples of our Jerusalem.

> So it was, as the multitude pressed about Him to hear the word of God that He stood by the Lake of Gennesaret, [2] and saw two boats standing by the lake; but the fishermen had gone from them and were washing *their* nets. [3] Then He got into one of the boats, which was Simon's, and asked him to put out a little from the land. And He sat down and taught the multitudes from the boat. [4] When He had stopped speaking, He said to Simon, "Launch out into the deep and let down your nets for a draught." [5] But Simon answered and said to Him, "Master, we have toiled all night and caught nothing; nevertheless at your word I will let down the net." [6] And when they had done this, they caught a great number of fishes, and their net was breaking. [7] So they signaled to *their* partners in the other boat to come and help them. And they came and filled both the boats, so that they began to sink. [8] When Simon Peter saw *it,* he fell down at Jesus' knees, saying, "Depart from me, for I am a sinful man, O Lord!" [9] For he and all who were with him were astonished at the draught of fishes which they had taken; [10] and so also *were* James and John, the sons of Zebedee, who were partners with Simon. And Jesus said to Simon, "Do not be afraid. From now on you will catch men." [11] So when they had brought their boats to land, they forsook all and followed Him.   Luke 5:1-11

The "lake" is a parody of the masses of mankind (the mission field). The "fishes" represent the various peoples. I remember an English teacher who

was the first to teach me that there is a correct use of the word "fishes." It

was indeed plural but used when referring to more than one type of fish.

Oddly enough she used the same lesson to teach of the correct usage of the word "peoples." It is used when one is speaking of in plurality of more than one type of people.

God would not have Christians engage in selective planting of the Gospel much less making disciples. When selective evangelism is attempted it is sin. Jesus encourages the fishermen to go further out onto Lake Gennesaret not away from the fishes but closer to them. We must not seek to get away from peoples but closer to them. This is akin to going to the places where we have not been fishing for men, the denser populated and forgotten areas. It is also about fishing for men in different ways while abandoning selective evangelism. [IV]

In Luke 5 Jesus teaches those who desire to hear him, but it is a greater and more intimate lesson he presents to those who would be his disciples. He challenges the professional fishermen with his deity; omniscience (He knows all), omnipresence (He's everywhere), and omnipotence (He's all powerful). The same challenge he extends to us today – to know him and to make him known from our Jerusalem to the uttermost parts of the earth (Acts 1:8).

> O Lord, You have searched me and known me. [2] You know my sitting down and my rising up; you understand my thought afar off. [3] You comprehend my path and my lying down, and are acquainted with all my ways. [4] For there is not a word on my tongue, but behold, O Lord, You know it altogether. Psalms 139:1-4

God is omniscient, not because he is a mind reader but because we have no thoughts outside of him. In Acts 17:28 Paul declares "For in him we live, and move, and have our being; as certain also of your own poets have said, for we are also his offspring." He knew the response of Peter and the other fishermen before they spoke. He also knows our responses before we give them. He stands waiting for us to partner with him.

God is omnipresent. He was in Heaven, with the disciples, and in the water with the fishes at the same time. He is in our urban areas, cities, communities, churches, and homes at the same time. He is not only omnipresent. He is ever working in behalf of the world that he created and gave his son to die for. He is calling those who have already come to know him to join him in planting the gospel at the same time he is preparing the hearts of those he would have us to share with. He is in total control of everything that happens everywhere. After all God is God all by himself. God is all powerful. God is omnipotent.

The Sovereign God

Fishermen and their abilities	Sovereign God
Longtime fishermen- possible church members	Jesus – God in the flesh
Taught and practiced best fishing by moonlight.	Knew and teaches best fishing is by "Son's light."
Experienced by profession in catching fish.	Created and commands fishes.
Cast nets where they thought fish were	Knew and knows exactly where fish are.

God has spoken once, twice I have heard this: That power *belongs* to God. [12] Also to You, O Lord, *belongs* mercy; For You render to each one according to his work. Psalms 62:11-12

When Jesus shows up the fishermen were doing maintenance work on their nets. As professionals they were adept at mending torn and weak parts so that if and when they got a good catch of fish they would not lose it due to weak netting. They would do all within their power to keep fish. Even with the extra work the fishermen put in mending their nets, as they obeyed Jesus the catch of fishes was so great until the net could not handle the abundance. God specializes in turning our nothings into over flow blessings. There is nothing and no situation beyond his power. Part of the glory of the resurrection is an adjunct declaration of our Lord and Savior having all power. The same power that Jesus used as he begin to pronounce the Great Commission in Matthew 28:18.

What Jesus Offers

What Fishermen had	What Jesus Offered
Pessimism	Optimism (Romans 8:24-25)
Old Career	New Calling (1 Peter 2:9)
Professionalism	Spiritual Maturity (Romans 8:1)
Earthly Experience	Heavenly Wisdom (Ephesians 2:4-10)
Unproductive Past	A Productive Future (Jeremiah 29:11)
Sinful Men	Holiness in and through a Holy God (1 Peter 1:15-16)
Hell and what it offers	Heaven and what it offers (John 14:1-3)

The fishermen had worked all night long and caught nothing. Jesus shows up and the catch of fishes in the daytime overwhelms them. The same is true of God's power in salvation. It is also true in planting the Gospel among all peoples and growing/multiplying churches.

For by grace you have been saved through faith, and that not of yourselves; *it is* the gift of God, [9] not of works, lest anyone should boast. [10] For we are His workmanship, created in Christ Jesus for good works, which God prepared beforehand that we should walk in them. Ephesians 2:8-10

The fishermen exhibited obstinence to what Jesus asked of them for several reasons including personal unbelief, traditional and professional experience, and the challenges that come with major paradigm shifts. After all they were the professionals in their business. They had been working all night long and had nothing to show for it.

For 21st century Christians, Jesus offers the same. How do/will we respond? In general, Christians have had a similar unproductive experience when it comes to America's 21st century urban fusion mission field. I would also say the same type of obstinence has been shown when it comes to innovative Gospel planting. We have continually done the comfortable "look like missions" activities in the comfortable areas. Moreover, there is no church revitalization without revisiting current realities of a given local mission field. Financial resources should be a byproduct of making disciples not vice versa.

Our unbelief, wrong perceptions, and fears among other things have hindered Gospel planting efforts across the land. We have done church in the places, at the times, and in formats we have come to feel comfortable with while taking in a small harvest at best.

In effect we have continuously done the same things the same ways, while expecting different results. We have had a bank or shallow water fishing for men experience. To date the western Christian church has put forth minimal efforts, with minimum resources and got minimum results. God is challenging us to launch out into the deep and give it all we have; transforming lives, communities, urban areas, nations, and even the world.

> And Simon answering said unto him, Master, we have toiled all the night, and have taken nothing: nevertheless at thy word I will let down the net. And when they had this done, they enclosed a great multitude of fishes: and their net brake. And they beckoned unto *their* partners, which were in the other ship, that they should come and help them. And they came, and filled both the ships, so that they began to sink. Luke 5:5-7.

After being told to launch out, the fishermen are told to get their nets ready for a great catch as they cast the nets "on the other side of the boat." This does not imply a slow or minor change; but radical "all deliberate speed" change. Peter who became a focus of Jesus lesson responds to the challenge with partial obedience. The challenge was to let down all the nets, i.e. use everything they had on the other side. Jesus, God in the flesh, knew where the fishes were. God also knows where the people(s) are that will accept his free offer of salvation.

The fishermen's response was to let down "the net" on the side. Mind you the fishermen had spent considerable time mending the nets and they should have been strong enough for a large catch of fishes. From this we can see our best efforts without God spell failure. Our Christian response must be complete obedience to God's direction,   fishing for men as much in untested waters as we fish in the comfort of time proven areas and methods that yield limited results. In letting "our nets" down on the other side we must be ready to receive the draught of souls God has for the Kingdom. When we trust and obey the catch of souls is so great it creates a need for partnership and multiplication. Just as the nets got so full of fishes they begin to break, and the boats so full they begin to sink; so too will churches fill up and church multiplication movements happen.

Place Definition... What's what

Urban (metropolitan) areas are based around at least one core city with a population of 50,000 +. The Metropolitan area designation can be traced back to 1959. There are 381 such areas in America and 7 in Puerto Rico.

Micropolitan areas are based around a core city or town with a population of 10,000 to 49,999. The micropolitan area designation was created in 2003. There are 536 such areas in America and 5 in Puerto Rico.

Rural areas are open country non-core areas and settlements with fewer than 2,500 residents; areas designated as rural can have population densities as high as 999 per square mile or as low as 1 person per square mile.

There are two major drivers of the dynamic (not static) American mission field in the 21st century. Urbanization and Immigration have made and continue to make America like no other place on the planet. These two processes create an "urban fusion" mission field environment that should cause us to look at how we approach planting the Gospel, making disciples, church growth, and church multiplication. My assertion is that eighty-five percent (85%) of 21st century America is a part of or greatly influenced by urban fusion.

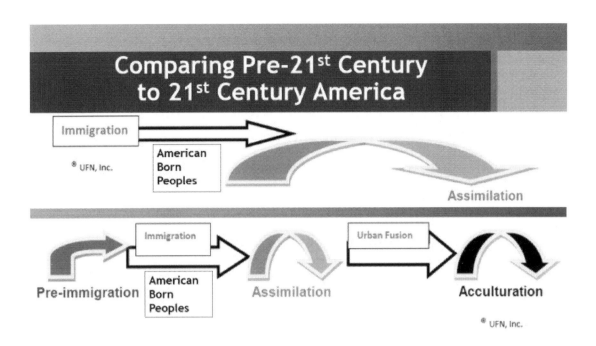

From its earliest beginnings through the first half of the 20th century, the American peoples' process involved basically immigration and assimilation of European Diaspora peoples to the legal exclusion of others (mainly Asians and Africans). The southern US border allowed for free flowing Mexican migration with little notice of the impending waves of Mexican and other Latino peoples to come.

It is important to also note that those peoples who immigrated in the 19th and half of the 20th century, "had a slow extended assimilation period" into an American ethos. Even the 21st century American Anglos are descendants of Europeans and others.

In the concept of urban fusion. I am saying the following: In the history of the world no country of worldwide influence has grown at such a rapid pace as America. Immigrants and the generations of immigrant families that have been born in America have been and are "fusing" at increasing faster rates. During this fusing, worldviews have not and increasing are not being maintained even within ethno-linguistic frameworks. Instead there are new worldview groupings that are more complex and can only be understood through different 21st century lenses.

It is important to note that I am not suggesting that America's ever increasing population is being merged into a country of clones. Actually, I am suggesting a much more complicated approach to worldview groupings. I am strongly suggesting that previous to the 21st century the American mission field resembled a checker game in its simplicity but now is more akin to a chess game. With such a complex mission field, Christianity's kingdom impact must be undertaken in collaboration

In the 21st century American mission field, a major demographic and generational shift has/is occurring. The socio-economic and political shifts of the mission field culture are easily apparent. Peoples are fusing. Racially diverse communities are on the cutting edge of social and political change because they tend to be bipartisan and more economically mixed. During the rest of our lifetimes, American mission field worldviews (ways of thinking) will be shaped by a mixture of continually morphing peoples dynamics creating unique "21st century American worldviews".

As the cultural distinctives in 21st century America are taking shape the Christian impact is lacking. For instance, a recent Pew Research Center report said that 1 of every 5 American adults across race, ethnicity and language identify as religiously unaffiliated. The number is even higher among those less than 30 years old. What will we do?

Christians should seek to have a decided biblical worldview as the common denominator in addressing the many mission field worldviews in 21st century America. A further course of action involves a collective Christian voice of diverse like-minded Christians within and across Diasporas framing missional responses to the 21st century realities of America's mission field through regular and ongoing interactive prayer, conversation and fellowship as we Plant the Gospel..." Together." To the extent that we frame missional responses in isolation, whether through racial, ethnic and/or denominational huddles we will continue to have little, if any, significant kingdom impact in America.

The American mission field is fusing across racial, ethnic, political, social, and community lines. These mission field rainbow coalitions create impenetrable barriers to the people group approach to planting the Gospel. An example of this mission field fusion is around the national debate related to gay and lesbian marriage. Those in favor of same sex marriage have no trouble "fusing" across all types of racial, ethnic, socio-economic lines. Christians are yet to demonstrate missional fusion around a biblical position of marriage.

Spying out the land akin to prayer walking and prayer driving in 21st century. Peeping out the land ... The area to be peeped is revealed by God thru prayer, meditation and affirmation among the leaders of the body. So when peeping takes place it's not a question of where but discovering 'the what' of God's activity.

Without physical evidence, and getting further away from a place, we are more apt to embellish. 6-7 ft tall men become 12-13 ft Giants. White picket fences become great walls of concrete... 50.000 Hispanics become 5 million Hispanics. Depending on what's in our pantry sufficient food becomes too little or too much food.

We cannot determine the level of the Christian maturity by how much lawn goes with the housing, how green the grass, or how many stories are in the structure. We can determine by how many vehicles are in the driveway or garage much less how new they are where the people are in Christ. At the end of the day we must understand the need for conversation and relationship. No one should epitomize conversation and relationship better than the body of Christ.

The Journey to 21st century American urbanization:

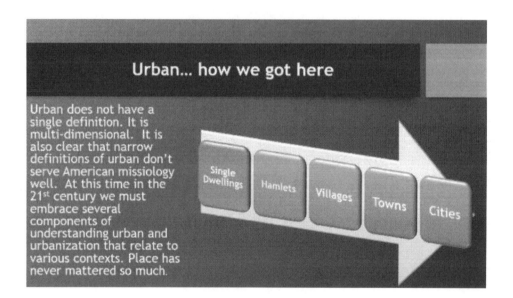

Towns were considered the devil's playground and the best thing for Christians to do was to stay out, only going there early in the day for the necessities of home (but even the country stores moved to towns) and health as doctors did fewer house calls. In fact starting with the advent of American towns, the missiology birthed in rural thinking strongly promoted staying away from these new gatherings of peoples. Missing from each of the development steps toward 21st century urbanization, has been and is an aggressive church presence.

In 21st century America, urbanization has escalated from the 20th century large towns and cities to the development of metropolitan or urban areas. According to the US Census Bureau update as of March, 2013 there are 381 Metropolitan Statistical Areas (MSAs) with over 250 million people representing over eighty-three percent (83+%) of the country's total population. Over 200 million people live in the country's 100 largest metropolitan areas (metros) and represent over sixty-five percent (65%) of the country's population. As of 2012, fifty-two (52) Metropolitan Statistical Areas (MSAs) have a population of 1 Million or more.

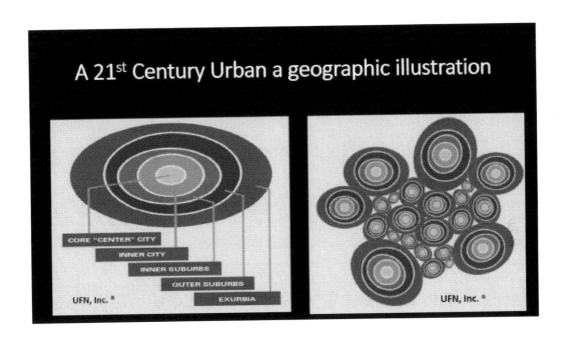

Metropolitan areas are made up of multiple urban cells as pictured above. For instance **in a given urban area there are multiple cells** so also multiple city cores, suburbs , inner cities, etc. not just one.

There are some stubborn facts associated with 21st century American urban fusion. I should state that my perception is that suburbs are not the antithesis of urban but rather a sub-part of urban. In the 21st century urban should not be looked at as inner city. The broader view will help us have better regional views of trends. Most people still have a view of the suburbs as solid middle class with very similar people living there. This is factually no longer the case. Enter urban fusion.

Poverty has moved to the suburbs of urban areas. The rise in poverty is not being caused solely by poor people moving in but a slipping in the economic status of long term suburban residents. Poverty grew by 64% in the suburbs over the last year alone. Today, more poor people live in the suburbs (16.4 million) than in U.S. core cities (13.4 million).[v]

Urban: A Demographic definition

Each urban area in the United States has its own contextual personality shaped by its historical development, the population growth of its indigenous and migratory peoples, and recent immigrants from around the globe. Most research agrees that over 90% of recent North American immigrants cluster in Urban Areas. Terms such as pre-immigration, assimilation, diversity, acculturation, and transnationalism must be understood as a new wave of affinity sweeps American society. 21st century urbanites embrace trans-cultural identity; l; and value living, working and playing in their urban fused environments.

Urban: A Psychographic definition

In general urban dwellers are highly sociable and highly mobile while indulging their preferences at a passionately high level. Urbanites will want to be active participants versus being passive by-standers. In urban attitudes we find peoples who are: strongly independent, young or young at heart, hustling entrepreneurial spirit, embracing the unconventional, and valuing discovery/ investigation they do or engaged in themselves.

Urban: A Conversational definition

News and Weather anchors in describing areas of their coverage region use the word urban over against suburban. In general, people in a manner of speaking but not with much thought use urban in attempts to be hip or cool. The word gets attached to clothing stores, specialty furniture shops and fast food hang outs. Of course, this all follows an earlier historical use of the word "urban" being synonymous with African American or poor city dwellers. For some sociologists, urban planners, demographers, and others who follow the world wide change to an urbanized society such uses of the word urban is troubling. They feel as if it represents a limited understanding of civilization's progression at best or at worst an arrogant denial of the face of a changing urban influenced world.

Urban: the influence of Mindset

The most important aspect of 21st century urbanization is its influence on the whole of American culture. All of the previously listed aspects of urban are limited in their reach. The urban mindset has been, is and will be

For some time to come the single most dominating component of the American mission field. Urban influence can be felt from New York City,

New York to Widener, Arkansas. Sub-culturally every aspect of American life from education, socio-economics, music, literature, fashion, ecology,

sports especially teams and many other areas of life informs the 21st century world views with which we are confronted. Something is in the cultural water and it is urbanization. Just as water is a commonality of man and creation's existence, urbanization has gotten in the mainstream and must be understood if we are to be effective in the Christian kingdom enterprise.

Urban: what it is not

Urban is and has come to mean much more than "city." While the word urban is derived from "urbanus – city living or from the city; in the 21st century even cities have become sub-parts of an increasingly urban American society. Urban is not limited to a racial group i.e. African American. To equate urban with Black Americans is racial profiling in a sense. Urban is not limited to a socio-economic group i.e. the urban poor. Urban is not a single system but a myriad of systems.

Urban is not limited to a developmental area i.e. inner city. Urban is not just hip hop. It is also contemporary classical music. Urban is not limited to a directional geography i.e. Mid-Atlantic or North East. Urban is not limited to a place in time i.e. 1970-1980 but is constantly evolving at an ever increasing pace to more and more dominance of American thoughts. Urban is not rural, and urban is not a passing fad.

Defining our Jerusalem

Why is designating a Jerusalem important?

1) If you aim for nothing you will hit it every time.
2) Knowing how to pray for a given local church field.
3) Aligning with God as the God of specificity.

There is the concept of Jerusalem as a connected development area even in New Testament days of Jesus' ministry:

> ....And when he was come nigh, even now at the descent of the mount of Olives, the whole multitude of the disciples began to rejoice and praise God with a loud voice for all the mighty works that they had seen; Luke 19:37

> And when he was come near, he beheld the city (Jerusalem), and wept over it, Saying, If thou hadst known, even thou, at least in this thy day, the things which belong unto thy peace! but now they are hid from thine eyes. For the days shall come upon thee, that thine enemies shall cast a trench about thee, and compass thee round, and keep thee in on every side, And shall lay thee even with the ground, and thy children within thee; and they shall not leave in thee one stone upon another; because thou knewest not the time of thy visitation. Luke 19:41-44

Define geography - determine the southern-northern-eastern and western parameters of local kingdom focus and impact.

In Acts 1:8 fashion the geographic Jerusalem has these parameters:

- **North**
- **South**
- **East**
- **West**

What is your Jerusalem?

Sometimes parameters are naturally set - high rise, rural village, and various multihousing communities.

Sometimes geographic barriers - interstate or major highways, water bodies, or mountains set obvious boundaries. We can also consider census bureau tracts, zip codes, local government zones, state government districts, or federal government districts.

Detail or Discover mission field entry points through:

- Praying
- Prayer Driving
- Prayer Walking

We can use the Google earth application to get an over-view of the area.

Always do a firsthand survey of proposed Jerusalem parameters. Visually survey the area by walking and riding to see what's in the community (minimally daytime, evening, and weekend to get real flavor of peoples) Yes three different survey times of the same area.

Discern what God is doing already in the mission field.

3 X 3 mission field Surveying

- 3 different days
- 3 different times of day
- Minimally through 3 sets of eyes

But ye shall receive power, after that the Holy Ghost is come upon you: and **ye shall be witnesses unto me both in Jerusalem**, and in all Judæa, and in Samaria, and unto the uttermost part of the earth.   (Acts 1:8)

A **geographic** consideration of Acts 1:8 missional context

- **Jerusalem - Local mission field**
- Judea - Extended mission field
- Samaria - National mission field

- Uttermost - Worldwide mission field

An important understanding of Acts 1:8 is that it is to be carried out among all peoples at the same time in all geographies. This means as we go about making disciples, we should do so among peoples who are like us and unlike us in our Jerusalem, from Judea, Samaria, and even the uttermost parts of the world.

An **affinity** consideration of Acts 1:8 missional context

- **Jerusalem – family, friends, and other concentric circles of connections**
- Judaea - neighborhood and work environment
- Samaria - people encountered but outside of concentric circles
- Uttermost - Internet connections

Observe other local churches or social organizations activities.

- What are the positive community establishments – schools, banks, stores, restaurants, community centers, etc.
- What are the negative community influences – bars, alcohol stores, palm readers/spiritual advisors, pawn shops, porn shops, drug houses, etc.
- What significant public/private/event oriented buildings increase activity

At this point how is my Jerusalem reflected in my faith community?

- Who attends my church???
- What types of housing developments do they live in?
- What percentage of people travel more than ten (10) miles?
- What percentage of people travel less than five (5) miles? ten (10) miles?

- Who are the lost/unchurched in my Family?
  Spouse__ Children___ Siblings___Uncles/Aunts___Cousins___

- Who are the lost/unchurched in my neighborhood?
  Immediate neighbors_____ Extended neighbors_____

- Who are the lost/unchurched on my job?
  Owners of business_____ Supervisors_____ staff_____
  Colleagues/Co- workers_____Contractors/Vendors/support

- What is the Racial/cultural/ethnic make-up of my church?
- What socio-economic groups are found within my church?
- Are there new and emerging peoples, population segments, or environments in my neighborhood?
- Who are the elected officials that serve the Jerusalem?
- Who are the grass roots leaders/influencers in your Jerusalem?
- Who are potential community partners who don't go against your core values within the Jerusalem?
- Who are possible kingdom partners within your Jerusalem? From outside Jerusalem?

A local church should make a bold declaration about the Jerusalem area for kingdom impact. Jerusalem parameters should be somewhat regularly considered in the context of the ministry and the mission field.

Chapter Four

M.A.P.P.I.N.G.
Interests and Needs

Then Caleb quieted the people before Moses, and said, "Let us go up at once and take possession, for we are well able to overcome it." But the men who had gone up with him said, "We are not able to go up against the people, for they *are* stronger than we." And they gave the children of Israel a bad report of the land which they had spied out, saying, "The land through which we have gone as spies *is* a land that devours its inhabitants, and all the people whom we saw in it *are* men of *great* stature. [33] There we saw the giants (the descendants of Anak came from the giants); and we were like grasshoppers in our own sight, and so we were in their sight."
Numbers 13: 30-33 NKJV

While field surveying looks at peoples and places; community assessments look at interests in needs. Community assessments[vi] are hard work, but failing to conduct a community assessment is time-wasting, presumptuous, and unwise. The benefits of a community needs assessment go far beyond information obtained. Planners can learn from the experiences of others, build relationships critical to forming a long-term local support group, and be assured that 'wisdom is found in those who take advice.' (Proverbs 13:10)." The involvement of church lay persons in a one day effort makes a community needs assessment very unique and practical. In teams of two, volunteers will visit, by appointment, local agencies, organizations, and community leaders who provide services to needy persons and families in the community. Collaborating with other churches in doing community needs assessments builds relationships that can impact kingdom work for years to come. The assessment focuses on felt needs in the community. Assessments will direct and help churches do ministry:

1.   Identify community needs.

2.   Determine what is now being done.

3.   Build a team relationship with local service organizations and open doors for ministry.

4.   Involve lay Christians in personal ministry actions to meet the needs of people.

5.   Share the Gospel and love of Jesus with persons and families in need.

I. PURPOSE

A.   To learn about community services,

B.   To assess community problems and needs,

C.   To build relationships with community agencies and organizations,

D.   To discover how lay Christians and your church can become involved in ministry.

II. PARTICIPANTS

A. Local church Survey Director(s) and/or Consultant(s) from denominations and/or independent

B. Denomination missionaries (In a small county or community the sponsor may be the Ministerial Alliance or a local church.)

C. Associations, fellowships, networks from Christian life

D. Lay persons volunteers from churches

C. Service organizations and community leaders (interviews), including the following:

- Human Services
- Public School administrators (all levels)
- Public Health Departments
- Health Clinics/Mental Health
- Multihousing Managers
- Senior Citizen Centers
- Public housing Resident Councils
- Counseling Services
- Alcohol & Drug Rehabilitation
- Department store managers
- Manufactured housing communities
- City Mayor/ Council office
- Police Chief/Precincts
- Food Banks/ Food Pantries/ Soup Kitchens
- Police Precincts
- County Sheriff
- Fire Department
- Senior Adult Day Care/Child development Centers
- Crises Centers
- Salvation Army Centers/Boys and Girls Clubs
- NAACP/Ethnic organizations
- Shelters /Habitat for Humanity
- Others...

III. PLANNING

A.   Select date for the assessment project.

B.   Enlist consultant at least six months before project date.

C.   Schedule consultant for a 3 day visit in area two months before assessment date. Consultant will meet with leaders to assist with inspiration, motivation, planning, selection of agencies, enlistment of volunteers, and to help develop ministry plans and action.

D.   If there is a consultant, he works closely with the assessment Survey Director.

IV. PREPARATION ASSIGNMENTS

A.   Recruit church volunteers to conduct interviews in community agencies. Enlist twice the number of volunteers as the number of agencies to be visited. This assignment should be divided among the those who are committed to assessing the area.

B.   Make appointments with agencies, organizations and community leaders. The assessment survey director is responsible for this task. Each team will visit two offices/organizations. Schedule half of the appointments for ten o'clock and the other half for eleven. Send a letter of confirmation one week before appointment date.

V. DAY OF ASSESSMENT

A.   Provide continental breakfast for all participants.

B.   Provide Association's "calling card" for all volunteers. Volunteers will print their names and phone numbers on the cards to leave with the agency person they visit.

C.   "Field Interview Narrative" will be given to all volunteers. It provides suggestions for beginning and closing the interview. It also lists the questions to be asked.

D.   "Interview Report Templates" will be given to volunteers to be completed when they return from their appointments.

E. Teams will be given a card listing the name of the person to be interviewed, agency, address, phone number, directions, and time of interview. Each team will receive two appointment cards with agencies located near each other.

F. Typist to prepare the assessment report.

VI. SCHEDULE OF THE COMMUNITY NEEDS ASSESSMENT

First day:

8:30 A.M. - Continental breakfast

8:50 - Interview assignments made to volunteer teams of two

9:00 - Orientation

9:45 - Teams leave for appointments 10:00 - First visit 11:00 - Second visit

12 Noon - Return to complete written reports 12.30 P.M. - Lunch (optional) sharing time

2:00 - Consultant and typist prepare report. Print enough copies for evaluation session.

Second day:

10:00 A.M. - Evaluation and strategy planning. Consultant, lay volunteers, church leaders, denomination representatives, and missionaries will review assessment information, discuss community needs discovered, and outline plans for follow-up and ministry action based on identified needs.

VII. IMPLEMENTATION AND ACTION FOR COMMUNITY MINISTRIES

Identify the team that will lead in developing plans for the implementation of ministries in the community.

* Review the purpose of ministry.

* Write three or four objectives.

* Write several specific, measurable, and attainable goals.

* Develop action plans to reach desired goals.

* Secure commitment of resources

* Assign responsibility for implementation.

* Receive progress reports and evaluate results.

* Re-cycle.

* Celebrate.

FIELD INTERVIEW Narrative - COMMUNITY NEEDS ASSESSMENT

Introduce team and present "calling cards" with your names and phone numbers.

Share that you are one of many teams doing a community needs assessment.

3.) Say: "Thank you for your time. We represent churches who wish to learn about the needs in the community and how we can be of help.

Our goal is

- to build relationships with community agencies and leaders;
- to learn about community services;
- to assess problems and community needs
- to discover how churches can be involved."

(Ask questions...take careful notes ... obtain "quotes")

1. What services do you provide?

2. What problems

       A.) do you face as an agency?

       B.) and needs exist among those you serve?" (capture responses)

3. "What can a church, group of churches, volunteers do to help?" (List in order 1, 2, 3, 4, etc...)

4. "If you had an opportunity to speak, to challenge church people, what would you say?" (capture responses)

5. "May we have permission to pray?" (Pray for the person interviewed, the agency/organization, and the persons/families served.

INTERVIEW Report Template - COMMUNITY NEEDS ASSESSMENT

Date:

Name of person interviewed:

Name of agency:

Address and phone number:

List of names of team members making interview:

1. What did you learn about the agency and its services?

2. What did you learn about the problems the agency faces? What are problems and needs in the community and among those served by the agency? (capture responses)

3. List in numerical order possible areas where volunteers are needed in existing services and programs. List also, services and ministries which need to be implemented by a church or group of churches. Specify clearly what needs to be done. (List in order 1, 2, 3, 4, etc.)

4. What final statement was made by the person you interviewed? (Share "quote"

5. State briefly your evaluation of your experience in the needs assessment.

Chapter Five
M.A.P.P.I.N.G.
A Godliness Barometer

Since you have purified your souls in obeying the truth through the Spirit in sincere love of the brethren, love one another fervently with a pure heart, having been born again, not of corruptible seed but incorruptible, through the word of God which lives and abides forever, because "All flesh *is* as grass, And all the glory of man as the flower of the grass. The grass withers, and its flower falls away, But the word of the Lord endures forever." Now this is the word which by the gospel was preached to you.
1 Peter 1:22-25 NKJV

What is a barometer? Anything that shows changes or impending changes. For MAPPING purposes I equate a Godliness barometer with the handles toward a Biblical worldview. To the extent that we move toward or embrace a Biblical worldview our Godliness barometer changes. Changes in our Godliness barometer impact metrics of our missional scorecard. This is true individually and collectively.

With full ethnic, cultural, socio-economic, educational, gender, and other lens; outside of a relationship with God we have our own views and live on our own in a cold world. There are all kinds of urban fusion worldviews waiting to be confronted.

A sinners job description is to sin. From superstitions to salvation of works that guides good values and thinking, mission field worldviews cannot be the foundation for disciples. Only the Biblical worldview from God's word is the solid foundation. Languages and Foods, while they can be indicators are not world view determinants. Fads ... come and go but are the result of world views not world view determinants.

Race and or ethnicity alone does not determine worldview. This more true in America than any other place in the planet. It is true in New York City but also true in Beck Spur Arkansas. As travel, technology, immigration and migration continue to impact an ever evolving America.

So what is an appropriate role of language in framing a 21st century American missiology? Language is a part of the communications venue and it can be a barrier, one that we must cross to be relevant. Looking to the music industry, gospel or secular, we can see how the language barrier has been crossed in relevant ways. While language is a grouping distinctive, it is not a world-view determinant in 21st century urban peoples fusion.

Most accept the word "worldview" as having German roots. A worldview is a person's mental concept of the "big picture" of reality as shaped by beliefs and assumptions about God, creation, humanity, morality, and purpose. A worldview is the lens or grid through which we interpret the world, the universe, and every percept of what is right or wrong with a person, family units, cultures, and nations. A worldview is a comprehensive framework of beliefs that helps us to interpret what we see and experience. It also gives us direction in the choices we make as we live out our lives.

Questions that determine if a worldview is biblical?

- Is there a God and if so, how do I see and relate to him?
- What makes for reality?
- Who am I and how did I get here?
- Is there a reason and purpose for my existence?
- How do I determine right and wrong?
- To whom do I ultimately answer?

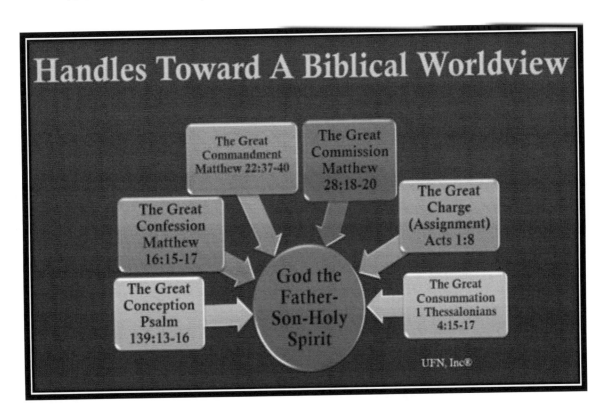

The Trinitarian God Head (Father-Son-Holy Spirit)

God has been an example of team and collaboration even prior to creation. One of the earliest biblical references to the God Head is Genesis 1:26.

> [23] Jesus said to him in answer, if anyone has love for me, he will keep my words: and he will be dear to my Father; and we will come to him and make our living-place with him. [24] He who has no love for me does not keep my words; and the word which you are hearing is not my word but the Father's who sent me. [25] I have said all this to you while I am still with you. [26] But the Helper, the Holy Spirit, whom the Father will send in my name, will be your teacher in all things and will put you in mind of everything I have said to you. **John 14:23-26 (BBE)**

> **[13] For You formed my inward parts; You covered me in my mother's womb. [14] I will praise You, for I am fearfully *and* wonderfully made**; Marvelous are Your works, And *that* my soul knows very well. [15] My frame was not hidden from You, When I was made in secret, *And* skillfully wrought in the lowest parts of the earth. [16] Your eyes saw my substance, being yet unformed. And in Your book they all were written, The days fashioned for me, When *as yet there were* none of them. (Psalm 139: 13-16)

You are no mistake or accident. You are even beyond intentional. You exist at God's direction. When does life begin? Life begins in God. You have arrived at a human existence through some incredible odds.

Greater chance of any of these happening than you being conceived in the womb:

- Man induced abortion during pregnancy prior to birth

- Winning the mega millions lottery
- Being Struck by lighting
- Being hit on the head by something falling out of the sky... you are not trash.
- A ship capsizing in the middle of the ocean.... You are not junk.
- Accidently falling out of an airplane... you are not an afterthought.
- Death by choking on a chicken bone
- Being hit by a stray bullet
- Being trapped in the Caribbean and a hurricane bearing down on you
- You are not worthless... in fact you are infinitely priceless.

If you go back 10 generations (250 years) the chance of you being born at all is **at most** 1 divided by 6×10^{100} or

1 in 60000000000000000000000000000000000 000000000000000000000000000 00000000000000000000000000000000000000.

In gambling, even a chance of 1 to 100 is not worth a gamble. Are you ever blessed to be alive!! The Psalmist speaks in awe of God's omniscience and God speaks for himself about his infinite knowledge in Jeremiah 1:5.

Before you were formed in the body of your mother I had knowledge of you, and before your birth I made you holy; I have given you the work of being a prophet to the nations.

... Simon Peter answered and said, **"You are the Christ, the Son of the living God."** Jesus answered and said to him, "Blessed are you, Simon Bar-jonah, for flesh and blood has not revealed this to you but my Father who is in heaven. Matthew 16:15-17 NKJV

A confession is an absolute acknowledgement of truth. After one embraces a confession he/she lives with what follows, believing in their heart that all is well. Peter's vacillation (Jesus rebukes him a short time later) after making the great confession reminds us that when we fall God expects us to get back up.

Consider John 6:66-70.

From that *time* many of His disciples went back and walked with Him no more. [67]Then Jesus said to the twelve, "Do you also want to go away?" [68]But Simon Peter answered Him, "Lord, to whom shall we go? You have the words of eternal life. [69] Also we have come to believe and know that you are the Christ, the Son of the living God." [70] Jesus answered them, "Did I not choose you...?"   John 6:66-70There are times when life's pressures can make it seem easy to just deny (in word and/or deed) being affiliated with Jesus. The disciples that stopped hanging with Jesus did not go back into permanent sin, but they relapsed. Some Christians today are busy in work for Jesus Christ, but they do not walk with Him. The one thing God desires of us is an ongoing relationship with Jesus Christ. We must give God a clear and open path to our soul to do whatever he wants. We should not try to keep ourselves in relationship with Jesus by any other way, but living a life of absolute dependence on him as much as possible. Never try to live the life with God on any other term but God's terms, and those terms require absolute devotion to Him. The certainty that I do not know but God knows all—is a major handle of walking/going with Jesus. Jesus wants to be our Savior and Lord, but he also wants us to be his partner in the kingdom harvest.

Neither is there salvation in any other: for there is none other name under heaven given among men, whereby we must be saved. Acts 4:12 (NKJV)

Where is salvation found? It is not found in our regrets or good works, because we could never be good enough to please a perfect God. It is not found in sincerity alone, because many religions and philosophies are sincere and yet diametrically opposed to each other and God's word. Where can salvation be found?

According to God's Word, it is found only in the perfect person and work of Jesus the Christ. By his perfect life, selfless and substitutionary death, and powerful resurrection Jesus proved himself to be what he claimed to be during his life -- the one, true God. Salvation is found in him alone because he alone is able and willing to save us from our sins. I confess Jesus as my Savior and Lord.

> [32]"Therefore whoever confesses me before men, him I will also confess before My Father who is in heaven. [33] But whoever denies me before men, him I will also deny before My Father who is in heaven. Matthew 10:32-33 (NKJV)

> ... "'You shall **love the Lord your God** with all your heart, with all your soul, and with all your mind.' [38] This is the first and great commandment. [39] And the second is like it: 'You shall **love your neighbor as yourself.'** [40] On these two commandments hang all the Law and the Prophets." Matthew 22:37-40 (NKJV)

In the 22nd chapter of Matthew's Gospel, Jesus had dealt with one school of thinking (the Sadducees), sending them away to ponder what he had said. He now is confronted by a lawyer representing the Pharisees. Jesus disarms this legalist and all other legalism regarding the notion that we can be saved by the law. Jesus, our Savior, was needed then and he is needed now as the way, the truth and the light.

A commandment is non-negotiable. Following this supposition "The Great Commandment" is a part of God's hand on the disciple's life. These commandments are not only non-negotiable they are from God himself. They are not to be diluted or tweaked. These two commandments stand as is. Isn't God awesome? He ministers to us along life's journey and then allows us to minister to him in authentic worship. Some may be old enough to remember various times in American life when different motifs for "who is my neighbor?" were more dominant than others. At one time who is my neighbor meant those who lived on the same farm. Then it meant those who lived on the same road. Later neighbors were those who lived on the same street. As multi-family housing began to proliferate, neighbor became defined as the person across the hall in the high-rise or in the same building. While each of these may have been/are cultural correct; they are all wrong from a biblical perspective no matter the point in time for usage. God would have us to know that any person of the human race is our neighbor and this is the biblical standard that we are to measure our actions by.

The mission field needs to know for what we stand. In general, western Christianity has done too good of a job letting the world know what we oppose. We don't have to compromise the Gospel to stand with God in love. When we stand for God in love we stand in God as we love people. There is a great truth in the song of the last century, "what the world needs now is love, sweet love." For God so loved the world that he gave his only son, that whosoever believes in him shall not perish but have everlasting life. God loves us enough that he didn't spare his son. He expects Christ followers (disciples) to love him with all of who we are. We are also to love other Christ followers (disciples) and those who have yet to understand the mission trip Jesus took from Heaven to earth. We show this love through intercessory prayer, living a life of obedience to God's word, and ministry.

"Go therefore and **make disciples** of all the nations, baptizing them in the name of the Father and of the Son and of the Holy Spirit, **teaching them to observe all things** that I have commanded you; and lo, I am with you always, even to the end of the age" (Matthew 28:19-20, NKJV).

A commission is when one or a group is appointed to a task or a function by the prevailing authority. God has commissioned the Christ follower and the church to make disciples.A series of "Alls" are used to give us the Great Commission.
1) "All power" - not limited to political, social, physical or economic power but Jesus declares that he has all power. Power to change circumstances and hearts.
2)"All nations" – Every person and all peoples are to be evangelized. God doesn't allow for

selective evangelism.

3)"All things" commanded – God does not allow for limited scripture usage and teaching. Jesus commissions his disciples to observe "all things" he has commanded.

4)"Always" with his disciples. This is a promise of presence directly from God. Not from man but from God. A promise of "I am" that means we don't have to wait to redeem or for redemption. He does not place this Godly promise somewhere in the future he makes it good right now. A promise of never ending extent. A promise of all circumstances. A promise of timelessness. A promise not just of old or tomorrow but of the present day. There is no place or circumstance that can keep God away from us. When family and friends are gone, he's there. When enemies seem to prevail or leave he's still there. God's commissioned expectation has not and will not change.

Making disciples is more than just sowing the Gospel. Making disciples is so much more than being a religious funding mechanism. Making disciples is not about creating strong members of one political party or another. Making disciples, who are being taught "all things that Jesus commanded," means that every new disciple embraces being conformed to Christ likeness. Each disciple embraces a customized transformation journey to eternity.

There are many good things that Christ followers and the church have evolved into doing in the 21st century and in some cases we have made these activities the main thing. There should be only one purpose for the Christ follower individually and in community. The one commissioned purpose is to make disciples. All else that we dare to do should be a means to this end.

Let's confess and repent over how we have allowed making disciples to get reduced to a part of the Kingdom enterprise instead of being the Kingdom enterprise. When disciple making is reduced to a segment it loses its rightful place as the umbrella for the other components. When disciple making is made a program it is minimized to classes, lectures and booklets. A disciple making lifestyle opens conversations for growth at all levels of Christian maturity.

Disciples are empowered by God through the Holy Spirit to teach. This does not mean that every born again believer should be able to step into the middle of a seminary level theological dialogue. It does mean that every believer is endowed with a testimony (a story) that no one else has. My story, like yours and all other Christ followers contains unique moments of truth that God has chosen to unveil through my following him. Every disciple should tell their testimony at every opportunity; God uses our sharing to multiply his message of love in America.

We celebrate what we measure. Baptism comes after the discipleship commitment, anything before this commitment is water play. Every baptism is a public witness of life transformation. Christian converts, where possible, should always be given the opportunity to have the family of God celebrate with them as they symbolize arising in the newness of life.

The Great Commission also embodies a tremendous promise. The promise is that our Lord will be with us always in every way and every place for the duration of the commission. So look back, he is in your past. Consider right now, he is with you in the present. With hope directly from God, look forward, he is already in your future, waiting on you.

A "Great Amen" closes the Great Commission. A closing of so it shall be done, affirmation, and agreement. The writer of this scripture would admonish us not to forget the Amen when God speaks. The great Commission closes with a "GREAT AMEN".

"You shall receive power when the Holy Spirit has come upon you; and you shall **be witnesses to Me in Jerusalem, and in all Judea and Samaria, and to the end of the earth**" (Acts 1:8, NKJV).

A charge is to assign a duty or responsibility to a person or to several people individually. Intermediate success should not interfere with our primary assignment. We often are able to see God do miraculous things as we are carrying out our assignment. Acts 1:8 is an assignment to the disciple and a synergistic collaboration to the body of Christ. Being a witness does not mean we are to convince people of God's reality. God does that himself. We are to be witnesses telling what the Lord has done in and for us (testimonies). Our greatest witnessing is the power of a transformed life.

The Acts 1:8 charge is geographic in regard to the world, from our backyards to the other side of the globe. In the American mission field we also have Acts 1:8 in urban fusion as peoples have immigrated from without and migrated within; global mission challenges are also within our nation's borders.

Acts 1:8 points out that the Holy Spirit has an empowering ministry. He directs us to where God would have us to be witnesses. He directs us to who God would have us to share a witness. He will also quicken us as to how we should share out of past experience, past equipping, and/or fresh encounters. As we pray and are sensitive to God's day to day; season to season; and life's journey directions we fulfill our assigned role in disciple making.

As in other parts of the New Testament, the Great Assignment is both historical and prophetic. It was for the Apostles and other early Christ followers as much as it is for you and me as disciples today. The Great Charge is also a witness of action and words.

The Great Charge is a specific and personal assignment to the believer. It is not to be delegated or vicariously carried out through resourcing another person alone. We also need not miss that the Great Charge is to be carried out in collaboration with other disciples. While we may never set foot in the ends of the earth, we can touch those areas through prayer and resource sharing. Modern technology provides a means for us to be even more engage when one considers resources like improvements in air transportation quickness and safety as well as Google earth and voice as connecting and prayer resources.

We should support others in the Kingdom enterprise but not to the exclusion of the Lord's direct assignment to each of us. Acts 1:8 is corporate in as much as when individual disciples are obedient in fulfilling it the local church as well as the larger body of Christ is more and more robust.

> [15] For this we say unto you by the word of the Lord, that we which are alive and remain unto the coming of the Lord shall not prevent them which are asleep. [16] **For the Lord himself shall descend from heaven with a shout, with the voice of the archangel, and with the trump of God**: and the dead in Christ shall rise first:
>
> [17] Then we which are alive and remain shall be caught up together with them in the clouds, to meet the Lord in the air: and so shall we ever be with the Lord.   (1 Thessalonians 4:15-17)

We will be brought into the house ...I don't know exactly where the new Heaven will be, but I will be there with him in my Father's house.

> In My Father's house are many mansions; if *it were* not *so,* I would have told you. I go to prepare a place for you. [3] And if I go and prepare a place for you, I will come again and receive you to myself; that where I am, *there* you may be also. [4] And where I go you know, and the way you know." [5] Thomas said to Him, "Lord, we do not know where you

are going, and how can we know the way?" [6] Jesus said to him, "I am the way, the truth, and the life. No one comes to the Father except through me. John 14:2-6

We will be alive forevermore... I will be with God in the new Heaven forever...

Now I saw a new heaven and a new earth, for the first heaven and the first earth had passed away. Also there was no more sea. [2] Then I, John, saw the holy city, New Jerusalem, coming down out of heaven from God, prepared as a bride adorned for her husband. [3] And I heard a loud voice from heaven saying, "Behold, the tabernacle of God *is* with men, and He will dwell with them, and they shall be His people. God Himself will be with them *and be* their God. [4] And God will wipe away every tear from their eyes; there shall be no more death, nor sorrow, nor crying. There shall be no more pain, for the former things have passed away." Revelation 21:1-4

We will be brand new forever...

[50] Now this I say, brethren, that flesh and blood cannot inherit the kingdom of God; nor does corruption inherit incorruption. [51] Behold, I tell you a mystery: We shall not all sleep, but we shall all be changed— [52] in a moment, in the twinkling of an eye, at the last trumpet. For the trumpet will sound, and the dead will be raised incorruptible, and we shall be changed. [53] For this corruptible must put on incorruption, and this mortal must put on immortality. [54] So when this corruptible has put on incorruption, and this mortal has put on immortality, then shall be brought to pass the saying that is written: "Death is swallowed up in victory." [55] "O Death, where is your sting? O Hades, where is your victory?" [56] The sting of death is sin, and the strength of sin is the law. [57] But thanks be to God, who gives us the victory through our Lord Jesus Christ. [58] Therefore, my beloved brethren, be steadfast, immovable, always abounding in the work of the Lord, knowing that your labor is not in vain in the Lord. 1 Corinthians 15: 50-58

Appendix

- Sources of information

- Local Church Jerusalem Definition Questions

- Jerusalem Vision Tour over-view

- Local Church Jerusalem Check list

- Missional Scorecard Template

- Glossary of Relevant Terms

Sources of Information

Websites:

- American Religion Data Archives – www.thearda.com
- Central Intelligence Agency Fact book online – www.cia.gov/cia/publications/factbook/
- City/Community Information – www.usacitylink.com
- City/community Information - www.city-data.com
- Federal Bureau of Investigation (FBI) Uniform Crime Reports – www.fbi.gov
- Google Earth - www.google.com/earth/download
- Information on Homosexuals and Lesbians – www.gaydemographics.org
- Information on Pagans, Covens, Wicca, etc. – www.witchvox.com
- Policom Corporation Maps and Economic Analysis - www.policom.com
- US Census Bureau – www.census.gov
- US Department of Homeland Security - www.dhs.gov/yearbook-immigration-statistics
- US Department of Housing and Urban Development (HUD) – www.hud.gov
- Zillow Housing search – www.Zillow.com

Phone/Tablet/Laptop APPS:

- 2010 Census
- ArcGIS ESRI
- BAO (Business Analyst Online) ESRI
- dwellr
- Google Earth
- Zillow – interactive information on housing

Jerusalem conversations to have/ Websites to visit

- Local Planning/zoning Department
- Census Bureau Data Centers
- Local Post Offices/Postal carriers
- Local public schools
- Public Utilities (Water, Gas, Electric)
- Cultural Associations
- Law enforcement officials
- City/County Government officials
- Long term local business operators
- Active Grass roots groups

Local Church Jerusalem Definition Questions

What are the boundaries (North, South, East, and West) of the Jerusalem?

What are the area/community names of note within the Jerusalem?

What is the approximate population within the Jerusalem?

What is/are the major ethno-cultural characteristics within the Jerusalem?

What are the socio-economic characteristics within the Jerusalem?

What are the other evangelical churches within the Jerusalem?

What are the non-evangelical groups (especially non-Christian) within the Jerusalem?

What are the obvious God presence absences within the Jerusalem?

What are some obvious signs of social dysfunction within the Jerusalem?

What are the major education entities?

Are there government or law enforcement entities located within the Jerusalem?

Jerusalem Vision Tours for New Members

- Set aside an entire session of new member's orientation for new members to understand and see the church's Jerusalem Mission field.
- After a light breakfast (pick up bag) members board a vehicle, van, or bus and see the local field and an over view facilitated by one of the church outreach team members.
- A debriefing is done at the conclusion of the session to provide further sharing and clarity for future individual and corporate ministry.

Jerusalem Vision Tours existing members

- As many as possible within the existing church need to see the current realities of the Jerusalem field for themselves
- Members sign up in advance, with multiple tour opportunities.
- Church outreach leaders facilitate tours highlighting mission touch points within the Jerusalem.
- Jerusalem passport – develop a customized Jerusalem Passport booklet that contains the highlights of the local church Jerusalem.   To confirm the occasion and commemorate the tour provide participants with round trip Jerusalem bus tickets.
- Give the reasons to focus on a local church field Jerusalem also provide visual displaying throughout the church, on the internet, church media and social media.

General Jerusalem Vision Tour items

- Depending on tour agenda and traffic allow between 1.5 and 2.5 hours.
- Provide a briefing sheet about the local church Jerusalem.
- What do we look for? What is God saying?
- Jerusalem vision tours can also be used to develop Gospel collaborations with other churches, fellowships, associations, etc.

Local Church Jerusalem Ministry Check List

- We have consistent focused prayer in the DNA of our church body.

- We believe intentional Jerusalem Ministry is Biblical.

- We have or we are defining a local church Jerusalem.

- We have a local church process for exposing existing and new church members to our Jerusalem context.

- Our pastoral staff and local church leadership is committed to intentionally calling out Jerusalem missionaries during invitation time.

- Our local church is committed to commissioning and celebrating Jerusalem missionaries.

- We have a pattern of consistently celebrating God's kingdom work in our Jerusalem.

Missional Score Card Template

Kingdom Baseline Information: Empirical Research

- Population (Peoples, Generations, Gender, Race/Ethnicity, Socio-economics)
- SBC Family (Part of Kingdom) assessment
- "The Church" Kingdom assessment
- Other religions presence
- Societal Markers – Abortion, Crime, Divorce, Out of wedlock pregnancies, poverty, illicit drug use, incarceration rates, and segregation. There may be customized variations in specific markers for each urban area.

Missional Measurements: What We Celebrate

- Intentional Acts of Kindness
- Gospel Contacts
- Gospel Presentations
- Daily Prayer Warriors
- Regular prayer Intercessors
- Discovery/Exploration Small Groups
- Bible Studies
- Leadership Development small Groups
- Preaching/Ministry Points/Missionary outposts
- New works on way to being established churches
- Established Church growth
  1. Traditional
  2. Non-traditional (Multihousing, storefront, house, etc)

Benchmark Goals: (Discipleship is a continuum of spiritual growth)

- Active members (Disciples) of faith communities in SBC
- Active members (Disciples) of faith communities outside of SBC
- New Congregations (Church Multiplication) as result of discipleship over flow
- Measurable decrease in negative societal markers
- Identifiable Kingdom partner reconciliation

Missional Scorecard Definitions and Clarifications

Missional - The processes, patterns, principles, and practices through which disciples with a biblical worldview join God in his mission of building his kingdom of transformed Christ followers.

Gospel Contact – door hangers, tracts, conversations, etc that expose a person to the Gospel.

Gospel Presentation – sharing of the Gospel by whatever method leading the person to an opportunity accept/affirm Jesus as Lord and Savior.

Daily prayer Warriors – disciples who literally pray every day with focus.

Discovery Groups – small groups with an intentional outreach focus. Geared toward the lost or unchurched as a safe place to explore Christianity.

Missionary Outposts – an expression of "the church" for Gospel proclamation, salvation decisions, community presence, and possibly church planting.

Bible Studies – regular gathering for the study of God's word intended for discipleship growth.

Traditional local church – an existing community of faith that functions in generally accepted norms of church. Location, meeting time(s), leadership structure, membership make up.

Non-traditional local church – a community of faith that is unique in its meeting location, time, or membership make up (i.e. collegiate, multihousing, all members under 30).

Disciple - One who gives their life to Jesus and begins the journey of being conformed to his image. (Luke 14:27). Growing as disciple is a progression that includes failures.

New Congregations – communities of faith that can be in existing church locations or a new location.

Glossary of Relevant Terms

Acculturation - A process in which members of one cultural group adopt the beliefs and behaviors of another group or merge into a resulting new culture while dropping their own beliefs and behaviors in most cases as a result of prolonged contact.

Affinity Group – People linked by a common bond or a group of people having a common interest or goal or acting together for a specific purpose.

African Diaspora - People of African descent with a new residency outside the African continent are referred to as being part of the Diaspora. This includes, brothers and sisters now in the Western hemisphere, Europe, India and Australia. The dispersion and spreading of African people originally belonging to an African nation and having a common culture.

Agrarian – A society or lifestyle with farming at its center. Also see rural.

Assimilation - the merging of cultural traits from previously distinct cultural groups, but not involving biological interfacing.

Baseline – The starting point at a specific time for measuring or tracking kingdom effectiveness in a given place or among a specified people.

Bench mark – The highest level of achievement or goal expected or attained.

BUPPIE – Black Urban Professional person.

Census tract - generally the smallest division through which information is gathered by a national information gathering agency.

Center City (Core City) – The main city or municipality around which urban development has taken place. The Center City is characterized by government centers and central business districts and in recent years has been the focus of much residential and commercial re-gentrification.

Conurbation – a very large developed densely populated area formed when metropolitan and or Micropolitan areas through growth sprawl join together..

Culture - the behaviors and beliefs characteristic of a particular group or geography.

Current Reality – A snapshot in time of the Kingdom work in a given place and/or among a particular people informed by empirical missional research.

Diaspora – The dispersion and spreading of people having a common origin. In many cases the term references individuals who self-identify as having ancestral ties to a specific origin. From the word "diaspeirein" Latin for disperse, from the word "Dia - + speirein" Greek for scatter or sow and from the word "spora" Greek for sowing or reproduction and spreading.

Emigration – To move from one place or country to another due to extreme circumstances. In recent years has been used almost as a synonym with migration.

Evangelical - those Christians of **all ethnicities** who emphasize 1) the Lord Jesus Christ as the sole source of salvation through faith in him 2) faith and conversion with regeneration by the Holy Spirit are personal. 3) the inspired word of God is the only basis for Faith and Christian living. 4) A commitment to preaching and evangelism that brings others into faith in Jesus Christ.

Exogenous – A person or concept coming from or originating outside the local community or culture i.e. non-residents in the case of multihousing communities.

Expatriate - person temporarily or permanently residing in a country and culture other than that of the person's birth or legal residence. The word comes from the Latin **ex** (out of) and **patria** (country, motherland).

Exurbia (Exurbs) – The fourth (4th) rung of development in an urban area cell. As an urban area has multiple cells it can have multiples exurbs. It is categorized by spacious community plans that can have borders from the suburbs to the closest rural area.

Foreign Born – A demographic designation for those who were biologically born on different national soil than where they currently live. Born outside of the US or its territories.

Gentrification – The development of a long lasting infrastructure including street patterns and housing. In the earlier days of American settlement this meant clearing the way for growth, in more recent times it has come to mean establishing or even re-establishing the infrastructure of a city.

Heterogeneous – usually referring to at least two people or a group having multiple or many differences.

Homogeneous – All of the same kind in a major aspect of thinking referring to at least two people or a group.

HUPPIES - Hispanic Urban professional person.

Ideology – a body of rationalizations, theories, and intentions that are strongly held in the foundation of a person or people's thinking.

Immigration - the movement of a person or people from one country to another.

Inner City – The second (2nd) rung of development in an urban area cell categorized by older housing and building stock. In most urban population centers, there are multiple inner cities. In recent years many cities have experienced the most regentrification in the inner cities.

Inter-cultural – Relating to, involving, or representing different cultures.

Intra-cultural - To reach within one's own peoples and engage in planting of healthy evangelist churches (kingdom growth).

Key Influencer – a person in an urban area who has positional power, relational power, financial power or some combination of power venues.

Megalopolis - an extensive metropolitan area or a long chain of continuous metropolitan areas mixed with Micropolitan areas with a combined 10 million or more residents. Formally there are three such areas in America – Los Angeles, Chicagoland, and New York.

Metropolitan Statistical Area (MSA) - An area defined by the United States Office of Management and Budget as having at least one city with a population of 50,000 or more and having adjacent communities that share similar economic and social characteristics. The total population of an MSA is at least 100,000.

(Micropolitan) Statistical Area - as defined by the Census Bureau and the Office of Management and Budget, are urban areas in the United States based around a core city or town with a population of 10,000 to 49,999.

Migration – To move temporarily or permanently from one place to another can be within the same country or to a different country.

Mile Posts – Significant points in time that mark the development of a new church

Multicultural – relating to more than one culture. (See also intercultural)

Multiethnic - A description that can be in reference to an individual person or a group pertaining to or consisting of more than one ethnicity.

Multiethnic Church – Sharing (church) prayer, praise, proclamation, and power in the context of a local church among more than one ethnic group.

Peoples – A Biblical concept used at least six times in the New Testament. The 21st century description of the collection of mankind in the breadth of humanity category

Peoples Spectrum – A general over-view of how peoples can be impacted with the Gospel by understanding their common worldview associations.

Person of Peace – A person used of God to open doors. Can be either a Christian or non-Christian..

Population Segment – A sub-group whose self-identity can be based primarily on socio-economic factors, generational boundaries, religion, or other common interests. A population segment is a strategic grouping of people within whom the communication can move freely without encountering major challenges. The number of population segments is ever morphing and unlimited.

Poverty - In absolute terms, having income and/or wealth too low to maintain life and health at a subsistence level.

Preferred Future – A preferred picture of what is seen at a selected point in the future.

Pre-immigration – A time frame that has increased importance due to the fast paced changing world. Assimilation can no longer be thought of as starting when an immigrant arrives in America. Gospel planting strategies among the foreign born cannot ignore what happens prior to immigration..

Psychographics - Psychographics initially emphasized consumer's activities, interests, and opinions. Today, psychographics has broadened to include attitudes, values, activities and interests, demographics, media patterns, and usage rates (Hawkins, 1998). Because of this new, more extensive, definition, psychographics is able to more precisely define who prospects, clients, and consumers are.

Re-gentrification – The redevelopment of an area, city, etc. that was previously settled or developed and for whatever reason became blighted but through various economic and community redevelopment initiatives has become a thriving area again.

Rural Area – An area outside of urban development that may or may not include a city or cities but is at best sparsely populated. Rural places have populations of less than 2500 residents in the principal city.

Rural Mindset – The word rural can also a matter of mindset. The view of some people irrespective of the community they live in to default toward an agrarian worldview.

Subculture - a subculture is usually marked by some significant points of difference with the dominant culture.

Suburbia (suburb) – The third rung of development in an urban area cell characterized by highly visible resident communities connected to the center city by highways more than public transportation. Usually urban areas contain multiple suburbs. In recent years distinction is being drawn between inner suburbs and outer suburbs. As re-gentrification occurs some inner suburbs morph into inner cities.

Transformation - A marked change in character toward being more like Christ, desiring what Christ wants is top priority, and obedience to God is the default response. Can be used when speaking of a place as in a marked change of a community or neighborhood, etc.

Transitional Community – A defined area that has or is undergoing change in the predominant type of people living there (ethnicity, socio-economics, racially, etc).

Trans-nationalism - the processes by which immigrants forge and sustain multiple social relationships that link together their societies of origin and new settlement. The process is called trans-nationalism to emphasize the notion that some American immigrants today build social fields that cross geographic, cultural, and political borders.

Under-reached – referring to a geographic area or people who have a minimal substantiated Christian presence.

Under-served - referring to geographical areas and /or peoples with limited Christian access.

Unreached – referring to a geographic area or people who don't have even minimal Christian presence.

Urban decay – an intentional or unintentional process by which a city, or a part of a city, falls into a state of disrepair. It is characterized by depopulation, economic restructuring, property abandonment, high unemployment, fragmented families, political disenfranchisement, crime, and desolate and unfriendly urban landscapes.

Urban sprawl – The uncontrolled and possibly unplanned geographic spreading of urban development to areas previously not urban.

Urban Systems – Urban challenges are multifaceted and cannot be understood or solved within the confines of an individual discipline. An appreciation of issues related to the urban environment, health, housing, transportation and education is implied. Cross-disciplinary research is foundational to planting the Gospel in urbanization..

Xenophobia – The fear and/or hatred of strangers or foreigners or of anything that is strange or foreign. Word first regularly used in the early 1900s.

YUPPIE – Young Urban Professional of any ethnic background.

Rev. Christopher "Chris" McNairy is the Facilitator of the Urban Fusion Network. The Urban Fusion Network (UFN) is a national network of likeminded Great Commission Christian peoples, churches, fellowships, other networks, and entities who synergistically focus on planting the Gospel, seek to enhance disciple making, and practice intentional urban missions collaboration. He has written <u>Missional Urban Fusion, Planting the Gospel in the 21st Century America</u> and the workbook, <u>Christians Responding to America's Urban Fusion Realities</u>. Just released is <u>The Gospel and Racial Reconciliation, the 21st Century Baseline for a Long Way to Go</u>. He has another forth coming resource entitled <u>A Jerusalem Pattern, Giving Proper Attention to Local Church Fields</u>.

Originally from Forrest City, Arkansas, Chris was saved as a teenager. An ordained Gospel minister (1985); he has served in Baptist life on local church staff, association, and state levels in Tennessee and Michigan.

Chris also served in full time ministry with the North American Mission Board, SBC for over 12 years (2000-2012). He served the Baptist State Convention of Michigan as African American Ministries Leader 1998-2000. While serving in Tennessee (1988-1998); he served as Pastor of West haven Baptist Church in Memphis, Tennessee for 7 years (1992-1998); leading the church to start "Hope Centers in apartment communities" that still exist today as well as other innovative ministries. He speaks often in the areas of urban missions, Gospel planting and Diaspora research.

Previous Occasional Papers
"Mr. Chris Goes to Washington" – January 2013
"The SBC – How we are…How we need to be." June 2013
"Still afraid to have the race conversation?" December 2013
"Can we do the main thing?" February 2014
"Can you hear me now" June, 2014
"The Gospel – What is It? January 2015

urbanfusionnetwork@gmail.com

Conferences Offered by Chris McNairy

- Urban Fusion Weekends around the Urban Fusion Workbook – planned with local church(es), associations, conventions.
- Customized Local Church Missional Strategy Development
- The "Jesus Loves" Initiative – Pilot completed in conjunction with the 2013 Presidential Inauguration. Weekend style Local church conference now available.
- Building local church awareness for Church multiplication
- Churches that transform people and Places
- Intentional Urban Leadership Development
- Planting the Gospel in Multihousing Communities (Seminar Series)
- Principles of the Harvest
- Stewardship: Not Yours but You
- Spiritual Gifts for a spiritual body
- Reconciliation weekends

Current/Forthcoming works from Chris McNairy

- Missional Urban Fusion, Planting the Gospel in 21st Century America (2013)
- Christians Responding to America's 21st Century Urban Fusion workbook (2013)
- The Gospel and Racial Reconciliation, The 21st Century Baseline for a Long way to Go (2015)
- A Jerusalem Pattern (2015)
- Planting the Gospel in Multihousing Communities (2015)
- Urban church leadership Development (2015)
- Devotional - year long devotion around urban fusion mission topics (2015)
- Equipping modules to be available @ www.urbanfusionnetwork.com

Selected Bibliography

Allen, Roland. <u>Missionary Methods, St. Paul's or Ours?</u> Grand Rapids, MI: Wm B Eerdmans Pub. Co., 1962. Originally published in 1912.

Bonhoeffer, Dietrich, <u>The Cost of Discipleship</u>, New York, New York, .Macmillan Publishers, 1979 Edition.

Bounds, E.M., <u>The Complete Works of E. M. Bounds on Prayer</u>, Baker Books, Grand Rapids, Michigan, 1990. Revised foreword 2004.

Gibbon, Edward, Esq, <u>History of the Decline and Fall of the Roman Empire</u>, Originally written 1782, revised 1845. Available through various publishing outlets

Hiebert, Paul G. <u>Transforming Worldviews, An Anthropological Understanding of How People Change</u>, Baker Publishing Group, Grand Rapids, Michigan, 2008.

Klassen, Ron and John Koessler, No Little Places, <u>The Untapped Potential of the Small Town Church</u>, Baker Books, Grand Rapids, Michigan, 2002.

McNairy, Chris, <u>Missional Urban Fusion, Planting the Gospel in 21st Century America</u>, Urban Fusion Network Books, Lawrenceville, Georgia, 2013.

McNairy, Chris, <u>Christians Responding to America's Urban Fusion Realities</u>, Urban Fusion Network Books, Lawrenceville, Georgia, 2013.

Pfeffer, Jeffrey and Sutton Robert I., <u>Hard Facts Dangerous Half-Truths & Total Nonsense</u>, Harvard Business School Press, Boston, Massachusetts, 2006.

Silver, Nate <u>The Signal and the Noise, Why so Many Predictions Fail-but Some Don't</u>, New York, New York, The Penguin Press, 2012.

End Notes

[i] Words by Jennie Wilson 1856-1913

[ii] From Jesus loves DC and Jesus loves Mississippi Gospel sharing tracts. Urban Fusion Network ©

[iii] These Prayer insights gleaned over the years from various books and other materials read but most importantly from my personal relationship journey with my Lord and Savior Jesus Christ.

[iv] Chris McNairy Sermon Fishing on the Other Side of the Boat first shared West haven Baptist Church Memphis Tennessee 1996.

[v] Confronting Suburban Poverty in America, Elizabeth Kneebone and Alan Berube, Brookings Institution Press, Washington, DC, 2013.

[vi] This chapter on community assessments is heavily influenced by consultation work of Dr. Nathan Porter with the author in Memphis Tennessee.

Made in the USA
Charleston, SC
05 July 2015